Cross-Shattered Christ

Cross-Shattered Christ

Meditations on the Seven Last Words

Stanley Hauerwas

Brazos Press
Grand Rapids, Michigan

© 2004 by Stanley Hauerwas

Published by Brazos Press
a division of Baker Publishing Group
P.O. Box 6287, Grand Rapids, MI 49516-6287
www.brazospress.com

Second printing, June 2005

Printed in the United States of America

Library of Congress Cataloging-in-Publication Data
Hauerwas, Stanley, 1940–
    Cross-shattered Christ : meditations on the seven last words / Stanley
Hauerwas.
       p.   cm.
    Includes bibliographical references.
    ISBN 1-58743-131-9 (hardcover)
    1. Jesus Christ—Seven last words—Meditations. I. Title.
BT457.H38 2005
232.96′35—dc22
                                      2004013858

To
Peter Ochs

Contents

Foreword

A short book usually does not need a foreword, but when you have as many people to thank as I have, a foreword is demanded. First and foremost I am indebted to the Reverend Andrew Mead, rector of Saint Thomas Church Fifth Avenue, for inviting me to participate in their three-hour Good Friday Service. God knows what possessed Reverend Mead to invite one like me for such a high honor, but I am extremely grateful to him and all those at Saint Thomas for making possible my participation in their Easter observance. I can report that mostly the congregation stayed the whole three hours.

9

Paula Gilbert read these meditations and made some extremely useful suggestions. Indeed her influence goes well beyond her explicit recommendations. What she might regard as only throw-away lines have found their way into these reflections. David Aers, Greg Jones, Alasdair MacIntyre, and Samuel Wells made many useful suggestions about earlier drafts. I owe a particular debt to my colleague Professor Ellen Davis for her close reading of these meditations. Ellen made crucial suggestions about how the text should be rewritten for delivery. To the extent these meditations could be heard (and I was not able to follow all her suggestions) is due to Ellen's good influence.

I owe a particular debt to Rodney Clapp not only for publishing these meditations but for his wonderful suggestions about content and style. Rodney has been after me to write "a small book" and this is it. I have no idea if such a book makes financial sense, but then Rodney and his colleagues at Brazos Press (and Baker) do their work because they love God and God's church. I hope this book may be of some use for that project.

The title of this book is taken from John F. Deane's poem "Mercy" that appears in his book *Manhandling the Deity*. The first two stanzas of the poem read:

Unholy we sang this morning, and prayed
as if we were not broken; crooked
the Christ-figure hung, splayed
on bloodied beams above us;
devious God, dweller in shadows,
mercy on us;
immortal, cross-shattered Christ—
your gentling grace down upon us.

Readers of this book who are familiar with some of my past work may find a different "Hauerwas" here. There is no humor in these meditations. Though I think there is a deep connection between humor (at least humor that is not cruel) and humility, given the subject of these meditations I simply did not see how humor could be used. Nor do I engage in polemics other than to try to expose our presumptive pride. So these meditations are different, but I hope readers will find here the animating center that I hope has informed the way I have tried to do theology.

I have dedicated this book to Professor Peter Ochs. It may seem very strange to some that a book "so Christian" could be dedicated to a Jew. I told Peter I wanted to dedicate the book to him, but I wanted him to read these meditations first because, given their content, he might find such a dedication inappropriate and possibly even an embarrassment. Peter is a good friend and I knew he would tell me the truth. He responded with this:

> These seven words (dibberot) show how much you have been brought up not only to the Son's service, but also to Israel's—to His Flesh in both senses. May His resurrection shine in you as much as the unrelenting facticity of his death, which, I see, drives you past the human self-centeredness that envelops all of us in modernity, much of the Church and the Synagogue too. But of course we see the Light in you too, the laughing joy that is as much fully God fully human as the other, is it not?
>
> "Deep calls to deep" (Ps 42:7). To share with me and with the people of Israel the intimacy of Christianity's most intimate moment is not an embarrassment—except as much as any love is embarrassment. (As Rosenzweig writes, the call, "love me," embarrasses because it leads me to realize and to confess that, before this love, I was a sinner.) And this, as I understand it, is not a one-way sharing. We are loved and love. We were sinners and yet loved.

Such a response means I need to give no reason why this book is dedicated to Peter Ochs, who graciously claims me as a friend.

Introduction

"Mystery" is not a word I often use even though I am a theologian. Indeed, I avoid the word "mystery" because I am a theologian. To say that what Christians believe is mysterious invites the assumption that what we believe is not believable. In short, "mystery" suggests that what we believe defies reason and common sense. What we believe does defy reason and common sense; but yet I believe what Christians believe is the most reasonable and commonsense account we can have of the way things are.

So when I use the word "mystery" in these meditations to describe the Christian doctrines of the Trinity and Incarnation I hope to signal to the reader that reflections

14

on the seven words of Jesus on the cross should test our deepest theological convictions. "Mystery" does not name a puzzle that cannot be solved. Rather, "mystery" names that which we know, but the more we know, the more we are forced to rethink everything we think we know. So it is my hope that these meditations respect the mystery—a mystery apparent in these words of Jesus from the cross—our faith in God requires.

Put differently, I have tried to approach these seven words in a manner that refuses to offer any explanations (particularly psychological explanations) for what Jesus says to us from the cross. It is my conviction that explanations, that is, the attempt to make Jesus conform to our understanding of things, cannot help but domesticate and tame the wildness of the God we worship as Christians. Accordingly, I found the writing of these meditations hard and difficult. I hope that those who read them will find reading them hard and difficult. I hope that the hardness and difficulty is not due to my inability to express myself clearly (though I have no doubt that I have often been less than clear) but instead comes from how painful it is for us to acknowledge the reality of the Father's sacrifice of the Son on the cross.

These meditations are unapologetically theological. I am, after all, a theologian. But I hope the reader will also discover that the theological character of these meditations does not mean they are without existential "bite." I think nothing is more destructive for our ability to confess that the crucified Jesus is Lord than the sentimentality that grips so much that passes for Christianity in our day. Sentimentality is the attempt to make the gospel conform to our needs, to make Jesus Christ our "personal" savior, to make the suffering of Christ on the cross but an instant of general unavoidable suffering. I should like to think the relentless theological character of these meditations helps us avoid our sinful temptation to make Jesus's words from the cross to be all about us.

By calling attention to the theological character of these meditations, I do not mean to suggest that my reflections of Jesus's words from the cross are "smarter" or more "intellectual" than other interpretations of his words. Just the opposite is the case. I have worked very hard to avoid making my theological reading of the seven words a substitute for the words themselves. Theology is a servant discipline in the church that, like all such disciplines, can be used by those called to practice the discipline to acquire power over those the servant is meant to serve. As a result, what the theologian has to say about the scripture becomes more important than the scripture itself.

Theology is the delicate art necessary for the Christian community to keep its story straight. That story consists of beliefs and behavior that are actions required by the content of the story. The work of theology is, therefore, never finished. The work of theology can never be finished not only because we live in a world of change but, more important, because the story we tell resists any premature closure. That story, the seven words of Jesus from the cross, forces us to acknowledge that the past is not the past until it has been redeemed, the present cannot be confidently known except in the light of such a redemption, and the future exists only in the hope made possible by the cross and resurrection of Jesus. In short, at least one of the tasks of theology, a task I have tried to perform in these meditations on the seven words, is to provide a timeful reading of the scripture for our time.

In these meditations, however, I try to do no more than to elicit the characteristics of our time, a time often described as "modern." I did not want these reflections to be accepted or dismissed because of my understanding of what it means for us to be "modern." However, I cannot deny that these meditations were written with a certain understanding of the difficulty facing the discourse of theology in our day. In his book *Anglican Identities*, a book I read only after I had written these meditations, Rowan Williams observes that the question before theology in our day is "how a language of faith rooted in experiences and expressions of 'extremity' can be rendered in a bourgeois environment without self-serving drama." That, I believe, is exactly the challenge before anyone who attempts to reflect on Jesus's words from the cross. I cannot pretend I have been successful, but that is how I understood the challenge.

Commenting on the work of Archbishop Michael Ramsey, in *Anglican Identities* Williams observes that we must be on the watch constantly for the ideological bondage that threatens to take over a church-based or church-focused theology. I, of course, represent such a theology, and it would be foolish to deny that theological emphasis is well represented in these meditations. Williams suggests the only way to avoid such bondage is to remember that while the church may be perfectly the church at the Eucharist, its life is not exhausted by the Eucharist:

> there is a life that is always struggling to realize outside the "assembly" what the assembly shows forth. In that

18

context, theology requires the naming of "humiliation" in order to recognize the prophetic import of what it does in worship, especially when even worship in its presentation or structure at any one time may speak of injustices or betrayals of the gospel (as when the ordained ministry speaks of one or another kind of social exclusion, when ceremonial speaks of anxiety or servility, when language evokes alienating or oppressive images).

It is my hope that these meditations help us name the kind of "humiliation" that is at the heart of the Christian worship of God. I believe with all my heart that the constant temptation to betray the gospel, a temptation amply displayed by the history of the church, cannot be resisted in our day by Christians trying to imitate the false humility of tolerance. Rather, the only resource for Christians to resist the ideological distortions of our faith—distortions all the more tempting because to be "self-servingly dramatic" seems a better alternative than to be boring—is our faith in the God to whom Christ prays on the cross.

That God, the God who prays the Psalms, is the God, as Denys Turner puts it, who is "beyond our comprehension not because we cannot say anything about God, but because we are compelled to say too much." It is not as if we are short of things to say about God. But rather, we discover, a discovery nowhere more apparent than Jesus's words on the cross, that anything we have to say about God does not do God justice. The darkness of God, a darkness nowhere more apparent than in the cross of Christ, is the excess of light. It is not that "God is too indeterminate to be known; God is unknowable because too comprehensively determinate, too *actual*. It is in that excess of actuality that the divine unknowability consists." It is only because God is most determinatively revealed in "My God, my God, why have you forsaken me?" that Christians are forbidden from ever assuming they possess rather than are possessed by the God they worship.

The above does not "explain" my meditations on the seven last words of Jesus. At most I hope this introduction may help some understand why the passage I quote at length from von Balthasar's *Mysterium Paschale* in the meditation on the first word is so important for my exposition of the other six words. Indeed I am not sure I could have written these meditations, limited as they may be, without von Balthasar's extraordinary book. (I have drawn on a number of sources in writing these meditations, but I did not want to distract the reader with footnotes. Instead, I have appended a bibliography at the end of the book that credits the sources I have used.)

I confessed above that I found writing these meditations hard and difficult. I am not even sure what I have done are properly called meditations. They clearly are not sermons. Nor are they theology proper, but it is not clear if I have ever written "theology proper." But whatever these are, I hope those reading this book will discover, as I was forced to discover, how extraordinary it is that our lives have been redeemed, literally made possible, by the life, death, and resurrection of Jesus Christ.

one

The First Word

"Father, forgive them; for they do not know what they are doing."

LUKE 23:34

Recall holding a just-born infant, or think of an occasion when you cradled a sick and soon-to-die grandparent or elderly friend. We are drawn to embrace those we love, but they can be so precious, fragile, and beautiful that we fear to take hold of them. These cross-shaped words of Jesus, words uttered in agony, put us in a similar position. We are at once drawn to these words, but we fear taking them in our hands, realizing that we cannot comprehend their power.

To comprehend these words we rightly fear would threaten all we hold dear, that is, the everyday. Everyday death always threatens the everyday, but we depend on our death-denying routines to return life to normality. But this death, and these death-determined words, are not ordinary. This is the death of the Son of God, a death that encompasses death, challenging our assumption that we have or can "come to terms with death" on our own terms. To comprehend this death, to be faced with these words, means life can never return to normal.

This first word, "Father, forgive them, for they do not know what they are doing," seems to offer us comfort. Yet in *Mysterium Paschale* Hans von Balthasar reminds us that this first word from the cross was made the "first word" by virtue of a questionable attempt to harmonize the Gospels. In fact, von Balthasar argues that the first of the seven last words should be the only word we have from the cross in the books of Matthew and Mark, that is, the cry of abandonment.

However, to begin with "Eloi, Eloi, lema sabachthani? My God, my God, why have you forsaken me?" asks too much of us. What are we to make of such a cry if this is the Son of God? We cannot suppress the thought: "If you are the Son of God, should you be saying this? If you are God, if you are the Second Person of the Trinity, how can you be abandoned?" This is clearly a God with a problem. There is ample precedence in the Psalms for expressions of being abandoned by God, but we think the Psalms express our despair, our feeling of abandonment, not God's abandonment. We assume, therefore, it is not seemly for God to pray the Psalms. Confronted by these words from the cross, we find it almost impossible for us to resist trying to protect God from being God. Accordingly, we seek some way to explain how or why these words of abandonment could be uttered by Jesus.

Von Balthasar must be wrong. Beginning with Jesus's request that those that crucify him be forgiven—which we try to remember may also include us—seems to offer the kind of explanation we need to save Jesus from the absurdity of being abandoned. These explanations are often called atonement theories. Such theories try to help us understand why Jesus, the son of God, had to die. We think it is really very simple: Jesus had to die because we needed and need to be forgiven. But, ironically, such a focus shifts attention from Jesus to us. This is a fatal turn, I fear, because as soon as we begin to think this is all about us, about our need for forgiveness, bathos drapes the cross, hiding from us the reality that here we first and foremost see God.

Moreover, as soon as these words from the cross are bent to serve our needs, to give us a god we believe we need, it is almost impossible to resist entertaining ourselves with speculative readings of Jesus's words from the cross. For example we think what a wonderful savior we have in Jesus, who, even in his agony, kindly offers us forgiveness. Of course we are not all that sure what we have done that requires such forgiveness, but we are willing to try to think up something. Ironically, by trying to understand what it means for us to need forgiveness, too often our attention becomes focused on something called the "human condition" rather than the cross and the God who hangs there.

We can even begin to consider whether we need forgiveness when we did not know what we were doing. It seems Jesus does not understand that we, that is, we who assume modern accounts of responsibility, need to be forgiven only when we know what we have done. However, we give Jesus the benefit of doubt by acknowledging we often do things we should not have done and we may have had some vague sense that we should not have done them. So we probably do need forgiving for what we have done when we may have had some sense we should not have done what we did.

Our narcissism even tempts us to try to understand Jesus's death by analogy with other deaths. Deaths imposed by unjust powers. Deaths resulting from prophetic stands. Deaths that seem meaningless at the time but are made significant by later developments. Deaths that provide some hope against the hopelessness that our own deaths seem to make unavoidable. But Jesus's death is not that of a martyr. These "last words" from the cross are not just another example of truth spoken because nothing is left to lose. By allowing himself to be handed over, Jesus in his dying is not trying to give meaning and purpose to death. As Bonhoeffer observed, Jesus's death and resurrection is not the solution to the problem of death. Rather this is the death of the Son of God.

It is also a stark reminder that these words are not first and foremost about us, about our petty sinfulness. It is the Second Person of the Trinity who asks, "Father, forgive them for they know not what they do." The Son intimately addresses the Father. We look away, embarrassed by a love so publicly displayed. According to Herbert McCabe, these words, "Father, forgive," are nothing less than the interior life of the Triune God made visible to the eyes of faith. The Son asks the Father to forgive, a forgiveness unimaginable if this is all about us and our struggle to comprehend the meaning of our lives in the face of death. By this deed, by this word, Jesus rules out all speculative theories that seek to subject these words and this death to our understanding about what is required for the reconciliation of the world. In von Balthasar's words:

> Over against such free-wheeling speculation in empty space it should not only be remembered that God is in his (ever free!) sovereignty the absolute ground and meaning of his own action, so that only foolishness can cause us to neglect his actual deeds, in favor of scouting round for other possibilities of acting. But, more than this, we must state positively that to be in solidarity with the lost is something greater than just dying for them in an externally representative manner. It is more than so announcing the Word of God that this proclamation, through the opposition it arouses among sinners, happens to lead to a violent death . . . for the redeeming act consists in a wholly unique bearing of the total sin of the world by the Father's wholly unique Son, whose Godmanhood is alone capable of such an office.

Is it any wonder we find Good Friday so shattering? On this day and with these words, "Father, forgive them; for they do not know what they are doing," all our presumptions about God and the salvation wrought by God are rendered presumptuous. Moreover, that is how we discover that what happens on the cross really is about us, but the "what" that is about us challenges our presumptions about what kind of salvation we need. Through the cross of Christ we are drawn into the mystery of the Trinity. This is God's work on our behalf. We are made members of a kingdom governed by a politics of forgiveness and redemption. The world is offered an alternative unimaginable by our sin-determined fantasies.

Such a politics is not constituted by vague longings for distant ideals but rather by flesh and blood. Flesh and blood as real as Christian de Cherge, the Trappist prior of the Tibhirine monastery in Algeria. Christian and his fellow monks knew their refusal to leave Algeria after the rise of Islamic radicals in 1993 might result in their deaths. Anticipating his death—he was beheaded in 1996 by Muslim radicals—Christian left a testament with his family to be opened on his death. In that testament he asks that those who love him pray that he was worthy of such a sacrifice. He expresses the fear that his death will be used to accuse in general these people, these Islamic people, whom he has come to love. He ends his testament observing:

> Obviously, my death will justify the opinion of all those who dismissed me as naive or idealistic: "Let him tell us what he thinks now." But such people should know that my death will satisfy my most burning curiosity. At last, I will be able—if God pleases—to see the children of Islam as He sees them, illuminated in the glory of Christ, sharing in the gift of God's Passion and of the Spirit, whose secret joy will always be to bring forth our common humanity amidst our differences.
>
> I give thanks to God for this life, completely mine yet completely theirs, too, to God, who wanted it for joy against, and in spite of, all odds. In this Thank You—which says everything about my life—I include you, my friends past and present, and those friends who will be here at the side of my mother and father, of my sisters and brothers—thank you a thousandfold.
>
> And to you, too, my friend of the last moment, who will not know what you are doing. Yes, for you, too I wish this thank-you, this "A-Dieu," whose image is in you also, that we may meet in heaven, like happy thieves, if it pleases God, our common Father. Amen! Insha Allah!

Christian de Cherge is a martyr made possible by Christ's death. His life is a witness that allows us to glimpse what it means to be drawn into the life of God, the Father, Son, and Holy Spirit, the life nailed to the cross. To so be made part of God's love strips us of all our presumed certainties, making possible lives like that of Christian de Cherge, that is, lives lived in the confidence that Jesus, the only Son of God, alone has the right to ask the Father to forgive people like us who would kill rather than face death. That is why we are rightly drawn to the cross, why we rightly remember Jesus's words, in the hope that we might be for the world the forgiveness made ours through the cross of Christ.

two

The Second Word

"Truly I tell you, today you will be with me in Paradise"

LUKE 23:43

The silence surrounding Jesus's words on the cross annoys and threatens us. Engulfed by this death-determined silence, we find these words too enigmatic. How can we be expected to know what they mean? We long for more of the story so that we can better understand what is going on. Even Jesus's words to this criminal, words that come at the end of what might be thought a minidrama, do not satisfy our curiosity. Why does one thief taunt Jesus while the other seems to recognize who Jesus is? What does it mean to say these are criminals? Could it not be that they are zealots who sought to overthrow the Roman occupation of Palestine? Does the one mock Jesus because Jesus did not turn out to be the liberator Israel had long desired? Is this taunting thief like the two on the road to Emmaus, who have been told that Jesus no longer is in the grave, but they are leaving Jerusalem because, as far as they are concerned, this Jesus does not appear to be the one they had hoped would "redeem Israel"? After all, what kind of redeemer ends up on a cross? But if the problem is that Jesus does not seem to be the kind of redeemer Israel desired, what made it possible for one criminal to recognize that this loser hanging on the cross will come into a kingdom?

We are frustrated not only by the enigmatic character of Jesus's words from the cross but by the general reticence of the Gospels. We think if we only knew more about what Jesus was really like, what he really thought he was doing, that would surely make believing in God, at least the God of Jesus Christ, more intelligible. For instance, why do the Gospels tell us next to nothing about Jesus growing up, or his relationship to women? And then there are the parables.

If only he had explained what he was trying to get us to understand. Even when he responded to the request of the disciples for explanation, we are often as confused by the explication of the parable as we are by the parable itself. Because we know so little about Jesus, our imaginations run wild trying to make up for the leanness of the Gospels and, in particular, these words from the cross.

Yet I believe the reticence of the Gospels as well as these spare words from the cross is not accidental. Instead, that reticence is a discipline given us by God to draw us into, to make us participants in, the silence of a redemption wrought by the cross. In the world as we find it—a world that seems to make belief in God some desperate irrationality, Christians are tempted to say more about what we believe than we can or should say. This is a particular temptation for theologians, particularly theologians like me who are critics of the church's accommodation to the way things are, who too often seem to presuppose we know more about what God would have us be than can be warranted.

In his *Christ on Trial: How the Gospel Unsettles Our Judgment*, Rowan Williams observes that "God is in the connections we cannot make," a wonderful remark that reminds us that our desire to say and know more than the silence scripture forces on us manifests our uneasiness with the mystery of a God who would be known through crucifixion. Our attempt to speak confidently of God in the face of modern skepticism, a skepticism we suspect also grips our lives as Christians, betrays a certainty inappropriate for a people who worship a crucified God.

In the "Conclusions" to *The Varieties of Religious Experience*, William James wonderfully describes the presumption we—that is, those of us formed in the white heat of modernity—have about the world in which we find ourselves. James's description, moreover, I think helps us understand why we are so desperate to know more about the God we find in Jesus than can be known. James observes that our lives are now constituted by scientific assumptions that make it very hard to believe that, as the psalmist says, "the heavens declare the glory of God." We now know, for example, that our solar system is but a passing case, a local accident, in a wilderness of space and time where no life will finally exist. Whatever purpose our world may have, it is that which we impose. James observes:

> The books of natural theology which satisfied the intellects of our grandfathers seem to us quite grotesque, representing as they did, a God who conformed the

largest things of nature to our private wants. The God whom science recognizes must be a God of universal laws exclusively, a God who does a wholesale, not a retail business. He cannot accommodate his processes to the convenience of individuals. The bubbles on the foam which coats a stormy sea are floating episodes, made and unmade by the forces of the wind and water. Our private selves are like those bubbles—epiphenomena, as Clifford, I believe, ingeniously called them; their destinies weigh nothing and determine nothing in the world's irremedial currents of events.

We may be Christians, but we fear the habits of our imaginations, and too often the way we live betrays our fear that we are but bubbles on a stormy sea. The weather of an aimless universe produced us, and that same weather will kill us. We worry that we will die without a trace because there will be no one to apprehend or remember the trace we were. As a result we live desperate, deadly lives in the hope we will not be forgotten. We take comfort, for example, that we are citizens of the greatest, most powerful nation in the history of the world. Doing so, we are tempted to support exercises of American might and wealth that may be unjust but are assumed to be necessary to secure our nation's power. To be a citizen of such a nation at least suggests our

41

lives will not be forgotten. When the history of history is written, America, like Rome, cannot be forgotten; as Americans we will have a place in history. Is it any wonder that a people so formed believe that what is happening in this man Jesus's life is something about our significance? Is it any wonder that we find the lean and gaunt account of the life and crucifixion of Christ so unsatisfying?

Accordingly it is almost impossible for us not to identify with the thief's request. Please, dear Jesus, remember us. Insure that our lives will have significance so that we will be more than bubbles on the foam of life. Jesus's crucified companion, however, does not ask to be remembered so that his life will have significance. Rather he asks, as the Psalms have taught Israel to ask, to be remembered when Jesus comes into his kingdom. Such a request makes sense only if Jesus—a man undergoing the same crucifixion the thief suffers—can fulfill such a request. We desperately ask to be remembered, fearing we are nothing. In contrast this thief confidently asks to be remembered because he recognizes the One who can remember. How extraordinary. This thief is able to see and acknowledge that this is indeed the One to redeem Israel. Often in the Psalms the psalmist pours out despair, asking God to help. But just as often help does not come, yet the psalmist sings:

Why are you cast down, O
   my soul,
and why are you disquieted
   within me?
Hope in God; for I shall again
   praise him,
my help and my God. (Psalm 42:11)

This thief recognizes that this Jesus is God's psalm, conquering death by enduring death itself.

Moreover, this thief is right to believe that Jesus is about a kingdom, a kingdom that threatens the kingdoms of this world, built as they must be on the lies made necessary by our attempt to forget that we are creatures destined to die. "Do this in remembrance of me." "Remembrance" is the form an eschatological politics—that is, a politics of hope—must take before the cross of Christ. Such a politics is not some utopian ideal to be realized in the future; it is as real as the body and blood of Christ we receive Sunday after Sunday—as real as lives like Christian de Cherge.

Remembrance is quite literally to be re-membered. Through baptism we are given a new body, a body no longer isolated from the bodies that constitute Christ's body, and we are thereby made capable of remembering that we live through memory. Only Christ, only the Second Person of the Trinity, could promise to the thief and to us that today we will be with him. To be with Jesus, to be claimed by Jesus to be his friend, is paradise, for Jesus is the kingdom of God, the *autobasileia*, the kingdom of the crucified. We need to know no more than this. To be in paradise is to be "with Jesus," to be pulled into God's life by the love made visible on the cross. Our salvation is no more or no less than being made part of God's body, God's enfleshed memory, so that the world may know that we are redeemed from our fevered and desperate desire to insure we will not be forgotten.

Here, in this crucified Messiah, we see the love that moves the sun and the stars. To be "with Jesus" means we are not "lost in the cosmos," but rather we can confidently live in the recognition, with faith, that God is not other than the one found in Jesus of Nazareth. How could we ever think we need to know more than this thief? Like the thief we can live with the hope and confidence that the only remembering that matters is to be remembered by Jesus.

three

The Third Word

"Woman, behold thy son!"... "Behold thy mother!"

JOHN 19:26–27 (KJV)

Dante called Mary, "Virgin Mother, daughter of thy Son." Dante's description of Mary, "Daughter of thy Son," challenges any assumption that Jesus's address to Mary from the cross is simply an example of a son's solicitude for his mother's welfare. Jesus may or may not have been concerned that Mary's well-being be secured by commending Mary's care to the disciple "whom he loved," but we must remember that this saying from the cross is in the Gospel of John. This is the Jesus who, when the wine gives out at the wedding in Cana, responds curtly to his mother with, "Woman, what concern is that to you and to me? My hour has not yet come" (John 2:4). Jesus addresses his mother as "woman," the same address he uses to respond to the woman of Samaria who had five husbands (John 4:21) and the woman caught in adultery (John 8:10). That Jesus addresses his mother at the wedding in Cana and from the cross as "woman" at least indicates that this is not a sentimental appeal to his "mom."

In spite of the current presumption that Christianity is important for no other reason than that Christians are pro-family people, it must be admitted that none of the Gospels portray Jesus as family-friendly. In Mark, when he is told that his mother and brothers are "outside asking for [him]," Jesus responds, "Here are my mother and my brothers! Whoever does the will of God is my brother and sister and mother" (Mark 3:34–35). Nor should we forget in Luke 14:26 Jesus says that "Whoever comes to me and does not hate father and mother, wife and children, brothers and sisters, yes, and even life itself, cannot be my disciple." In our desire to make Jesus "normal," a man who liked children, we are tempted to forget that Jesus never married or had children. That he welcomed the children to come to him as manifestations of the kingdom may be for no other reason than that children do not have children.

I do not call attention to Jesus's anti-family remarks to denigrate his address to Mary from the cross. Indeed I think we can only appreciate Jesus's commending Mary to the beloved disciple, as well as his charge to the disciple to regard Mary as his mother, when we recognize that Mary is not just another mother. Rather, Mary is the firstborn of the new creation. Without Mary's response "Here am I" to Gabriel, our salvation would not be. Raniero Cantalamessa quite rightly, therefore, entitled his book on Mary, *Mary: Mirror of the Church*.

Cantalamessa, moreover, makes the fascinating observation that in the New Testament Jesus is often designated or assumed to be the new Adam, the new Moses, or the new David, but he is never called the new Abraham. Cantalamessa suggests that the reason Jesus is not associated with Abraham is very simple—Mary is our Abraham. Just as Abraham did not resist God's call to leave his father's country to go to a new land, so Mary did not resist God's declaration that she would bear a child through the power of the Holy Spirit. Abraham's faith foreshadows Mary's "Here am I" because just as we are Abraham's children through faith, so we become children of the new age inaugurated in Christ through Mary's faithfulness.

God restrained Abraham's blow that would have sacrificed Isaac, but the Father does not hold back from the sacrifice of Mary's son. Jesus's command that Mary should "behold your son" is to ask Mary to see that the one born of her body was born to be sacrificed so that we might live. As Gregory of Nyssa put it, "If one examines this mystery, one will prefer to say not that his death was a consequence of his birth, but that the birth was undertaken so that he could die." When God tested Abraham by commanding the sacrifice of Isaac, Abraham's "Here I am" (Genesis 22:1) did not result in Isaac's death. Mary's "Here am I," however, could not save her son from being the one born to die on a cross.

In the eleventh chapter of the book of Hebrews we are reminded that "by faith" did our foremothers and fathers live. Yet Mary, true daughter of Israel, was tested as no one in Israel had ever been tested. Jesus's "behold your son" asked Mary to witness the immolation of the Son, to enter the darkness that is the cross, yet to hold fast to the promises she had received from the Spirit that this is the one who will scatter the proud, bring down the powerful from their thrones, fill the hungry with good things, and fulfill the promises made to Abraham and his descendants. Her son, the Messiah, will do all this from the cross.

Jesus charges Mary to regard as her own, her true family, the "disciple whom he loved." Drawing disciples into the church, Mary shares her faith, making possible our faith. At this moment, at the foot of the cross, we are drawn into the mystery of salvation through the beginning of the church. Mary, the new Eve, becomes for us the firstborn of a new reality, of a new family, that only God could create. Augustine observed that the God who created us without us refuses to save us without us. Mary is the first great representative of that "us." Accordingly Mary, the Jew, in a singular fashion becomes for us the forerunner of our faith, making it impossible for Christians to forget that without God's promises to Israel our faith is in vain. When Christians repress the role of Mary in our salvation we are tempted to forget that God remains faithful to his promises to his people, the Jews. Our Savior was born of Mary, making us, like the Jews, a bodily people who live by faith in the One who asks us to behold his crucified body.

Jesus, therefore, commands the disciple, his beloved disciple, not to regard Mary as Jesus's mother but rather to recognize that Mary is "your mother." Mary's peculiar role in our salvation does not mean that she is separate from the church. Rather, Mary's role in our salvation is singular because, beginning with the beloved disciple, she is made a member of the church. Mary is one of us, which means the distance between her and us is that constituted by both her and our distance between Trinity and us, that is, between creatures and Creator. In Augustine's words, "Holy is Mary, blessed is Mary, but the Church is more important than the Virgin Mary. Why is this so? Because Mary is part of the Church, a holy and excellent member, above all others but, nevertheless, a member of the whole body. And if she is a member of the whole body, doubtlessly the body is more important than a member of the body."

So may we never forget that we, the church, comprise Mary's home. A home, moreover, that promises not safety but rather the ongoing challenge of being a people called from the nations to be God's people. A people constituted by faith in the One who refused to triumph through the violence the world believes to be the only means possible to achieve some limited good, to insure we will be remembered. The refusal to use violence in the name of the good does not mean this people can forget those singled out in Mary's song of triumph—that is, the poor and powerless. Rather, it means that such a people, Mary-like, must live by hope—a hope that patiently waits with Mary at the foot of her son's cross.

If this is not the Second Person of the Trinity, the One alone who has the power to forgive our sins, then this Mary-shaped patience in a world constituted by injustice and violence would be the ultimate folly. That is why it is so important that we not forget that these words from the cross are the words of the Son of God. The work that the Son does on the cross through the Spirit makes us the re-membered, God's memory, so that the world may know that there is an alternative to a world constituted by the fear of death. We confess that too often we forget we are God's re-membered, and that is why we pray "Hail Mary, full of grace, pray for us."

four

The Fourth Word

"My God, my God, why have you forsaken me?"

The horror! The horror!" Kurtz's words from Conrad's *Heart of Darkness* sear our souls. We, that is, the survivors of the century past, believe we know horror. World War I, World War II, Auschwitz, Dachau, Treblinka, Rwanda, Hiroshima, September 11, 2001. Names for death, endless death, that name our history. We believe that if we know anything, we know horror—the darkness hidden in our determinedly superficial lives, lives calculated to deny the darkness of our death-drenched time.

It is not surprising, therefore, that of all the words of Jesus from the cross, we most identify with "My God, my God, why have you forsaken me?" We do so because we think we have some idea about what it means to be forsaken. In the face of terror surrounding our lives, God remains silent. Though we are a bit embarrassed by Jesus (whom we thought to have some special relation with God) venting his frustration with being so humiliated, we nonetheless find this cry of dereliction comforting. Maybe God does understand our suffering. Maybe God even suffers with us, which some seem to think is comforting given the fact it is very clear God is incapable of doing anything about our suffering.

That we can even begin to entertain such thoughts is but an indication of our refusal, indeed our inability, to believe that this One who hangs on this obscure and humiliating cross is God. That this is God means Jesus's words, "My God, My God, why have you forsaken me?" are not words describing the horror we inflict on ourselves and one another. Jesus's words are not meant to express the anxiety created by the recognition that when all is said and done we are all going to be dead. Rather, if we are to understand the power of these words, these words drawn from Psalm 22, we must allow them to draw us into the mystery of the inner life of Israel's Lord.

It is not by accident that the Psalms are for Jews and Christians our prayer book. We pray the Psalms not because they give expression to our religious experience—though they sometimes may do that—but because our lives are given form by praying the Psalms. But in truth only one life, the life of Jesus, has been the perfect prayer the Psalms are meant to form. As those who have been charged to care for Mary, herself a Jew, we cannot be shaped by these words from the cross if we forget they are prayed by the One for whom Israel has longed. Only a people like Israel, a God-possessed people, can know what it might mean to be abandoned by God. This is not a cry of general dereliction; it is the cry of the long-expected Messiah, sacrificed in our stead and thus becoming the end of sacrifice.

This cry is but the prismatic exemplification of the love that is God's life. It is the love that was in Christ Jesus,

who, though he was in the form
  of God,

did not regard equality with
  God
  as something to be exploited,
but emptied himself,
  taking the form of a slave,
  being born in human likeness.
And being found in human form,
  he humbled himself
  and became obedient to the
      point of death—
  even death on a cross. (Philippians 2:6–8)

Jesus's being handed over, Jesus's obedience even to the point of death, Jesus's cry of abandonment makes no sense if this is not the outworking of the mystery called Trinity. This is not God becoming what God was not, but rather here we witness what God has always been. Here, as the Second Council of Constantinople put it, "one of the Trinity suffered in the flesh." The Word that was in the beginning, the Word that was with God, the Word through whom all things came into being, the Word that shines in the darkness, the Word that assumed our flesh, suffering even unto death, is God. The cross, this cry of abandonment, is not God becoming something other than God, is not an act of divine self-alienation; instead this is the very character of God's *kenosis*—complete self-emptying made possible by perfect love.

Contrary to those who suggest that only if God is capable of suffering is he capable of love, it is only because God is Trinity—that is, it is only because God is perfect self-giving, perfect self-same delight—that he can suffer as one of us. According to Michael Hanby, only because God is God, unchanging and ever faithful, can the Son be given over into our hands to the point of our ultimate estrangement from him.

Hans von Balthasar puts it this way:

> Simultaneously God the Father hands over his Son ("does not spare his Son"), thanks to his love for us (Romans 8:32; John 3:16), but it [is] also due to Christ's love for us (Romans 8:35; Galatians 2, 20; Ephesians 5:2) in such a way that in Christ's gratuitous self-gift (John 10:18) the Father's unconditional love becomes plain.

This is not a dumb show that some abstract idea of god appears to go through to demonstrate that he or she really has our best interest at heart. No, this is the Father's deliberately giving his Christ over to a deadly destiny so that our destiny would not be determined by death.

It is here that we see, as Rowan Williams puts it, "the sheer, unimaginable *differentness*—of God." "My God, my God, Why have you forsaken me?" shatters all our attempts to understand God in human terms. We try, for example, to compliment God by saying that God is transcendent, but ironically our very notion of transcendence can make God a creature after our own hearts. Our idea of God, our assumption that God must possess the sovereign power to make everything turn out all right for us, at least in the long run, is revealed by Jesus's cry of abandonment to be the idolatry it is. The god we assume is but a name we use to impose some purpose on what we otherwise think is blind fate comes to ruin in these words from the cross.

These words from the cross, and the cross itself, mean that the Father is to be found when all traces of power, at least as we understand power, are absent; that the Spirit's authoritative witness is most clearly revealed when all forms of human authority are lost; and that our God's power and authority is to be found exemplified in this captive under the sentence of death. The silence of Jesus before Pilate can now be understood for what it was—namely, that Jesus refuses to accept the terms of how the world understands power and authority. In truth we stand with Pilate. We do not want to give up our understanding of God. We do not want Jesus to be abandoned because we do not want to acknowledge that the one who abandons and is abandoned is God. We seek to "explain" these words of dereliction, to save and protect God from making a fool out of being God, but our attempts to protect God reveal how frightening we find a God who refuses to save us by violence.

God is most revealed when he seems to us the most hidden. "Christ's moment of most absolute particularity—the absolute dereliction of the cross—is the moment in which the glory of God, his power to be where and when he will be, is displayed before the eyes of the world," says David Bentley Hart. Here God in Christ refuses to let our sin determine our relation to him. God's love for us means he can hate only that which alienates his creatures from the love manifest in our creation. Cyril of Jerusalem observes that by calling on his Father as "my God," Christ does so on our behalf and in our place. Hear these words, "My God, My God, Why have you forsaken me?" and know that the Son of God has taken our place, become for us the abandonment our sin produces, so that we may live confident that the world has been redeemed by this cross.

So redeemed, any account of the cross that suggests God must somehow satisfy an abstract theory of justice by sacrificing his Son on our behalf is clearly wrong. Indeed such accounts are dangerously wrong. The Father's sacrifice of the Son and the Son's willing sacrifice is God's justice. Just as there is no God who is not the Father, Son, and Holy Spirit, so there is no god who must be satisfied that we might be spared. We are the spared because God refuses to have us lost. "The horror, the horror" is not and cannot ever be the last word about our existence. It cannot be the last word because the Son's obedience even to death means:

> Therefore God also highly
> exalted him
> and gave him the name
> that is above every name,
> so that at the name of Jesus
> every knee should bend,
> in heaven and on earth and
> under the earth,
> and every tongue should confess
> that Jesus Christ is Lord,
> to the glory of God the Father. (Phil. 2:9–11)

five

The Fifth Word

"I thirst."

JOHN 19:28 (KJV)

I thirst," says the Christ. "I thirst"? How can the Second Person of the Trinity "thirst"? Surely this must be meant metaphorically. But if this is only a metaphor— something said for our benefit to insure that in spite of being the Second Person of the Trinity Jesus tries to

71

identify with our lot—then the cross is just a cruel joke. What are we to make, therefore, of "I thirst"?

John tells us that this was said to fulfill the scripture. Psalm 22:14–15 reads:

> I am poured out like water,
>   and all my bones are out of
>   joint;
> my heart is like wax;
>   it is melted within my breast;
> my mouth is dried up like a
>   potsherd,
>   and my tongue sticks to my
>   jaws;
> you lay me in the dust of
>   death.

Some responded to Jesus's thirst by holding a sponge of sour wine on a branch of hyssop, recalling Psalm 69:21, where we are told the psalmist was given poison for food and vinegar to drink.

No doubt these Psalms shaped the memory of those who witnessed the crucifixion, but that they did so does not mean that Jesus actually did not thirst, that Jesus did not suffer. Jesus's thirsting, Jesus's suffering in accordance with the Psalms is a reminder that this Jesus is Israel's son. Israel's suffering, her abandonment, comes to a climax in the cross of Jesus. Finally in this "I thirst" we see the end of Israel's Christ-haunted sufferings.

Yet we continue to harbor the thought that it is one thing for Israel to thirst, but it is quite another thing for Jesus to thirst. What does it mean for the scripture to be fulfilled? Does it mean that Jesus's tongue does not "stick to his jaw"? Surely he did thirst, but we continue to be puzzled. Why, out of all the physical abuse of the cross, is thirst singled out?

Keep in mind that this is John's Gospel. This is the Gospel in which Jesus asks the Samaritan woman for a drink only to be told by her that he, a Jew, should not ask to be given water by a Samaritan. She also observes that the living water he promises seems quite unreal, given the fact he has no bucket. Jesus responds by noting that everyone who drinks water from this well will thirst again, "but those who drink of the water that I will give them will never be thirsty. The water that I will give will become in them a spring of water gushing up to eternal life" (John 4:13–14).

If Jesus just is this living water, how can he also be the one who says on the cross, "I thirst"? "I thirst" seems so out of character for the Jesus we find in the Gospel of John. The Jesus of the "I am": "I am the bread of life" (John 6:35), "I am the light of the world" (John 8:12), "I am the good shepherd" (John 10:11), "I am the resurrection and the life" (John 11:25), "I am the true vine" (John 15:1). How can this Jesus—the Jesus who seems so self-assured, so completely in control—thirst?

I think it is important to acknowledge we (that is, people with modern sensibilities) rather like the idea that Jesus might be thirsty. We think that if we had been present at the cross we surely would have wanted to give him something to drink. On the other hand the Jesus of the "I am" seems far too self-involved. We so desperately want Jesus to be an all-around good guy, but in the Gospel of John he seems so driven, so unlike us. "I thirst" is at least some indication that he had a normal, human side.

In Matthew and Mark it seems the dryness of Jesus's throat meant that his cry of abandonment was not easily understood. Some speculated that Jesus was calling on Elijah to come and save him. Elijah had been taken to God without dying, so it was thought—given Jesus's extraordinary claims about himself and his work—that he too might be taken to heaven without dying. However, because we, looking back, know Jesus is to die, we can feel quite superior to those who speculated that Elijah must first come if the Messiah is to appear. Because Jesus will die it is not that difficult to think he may have been thirsty, yet I suspect that our attempt to understand Jesus's "I thirst" as an indication of his "humanity" puts us in the vicinity of those who thought Jesus was best understood in terms of various theories they entertained about Elijah.

In truth Jesus's "I thirst" pulls us into the very mystery of the Incarnation. But to say "Incarnation" does not "explain" Jesus's "I thirst" from the cross. Indeed it is a mistake to think these great doctrines of our faith, the Trinity and Incarnation, are meant to explain. These doctrines are quite literally names for mysteries, that is, the naming of what is open for all to see yet become for us the incomprehensible salvation wrought in Christ. As Rowan Williams observes, we are tempted to make "Trinity" and "Incarnation" explanations because we want to "believe" in something external to us in order to forget "what profound and frightening differences in the human world they actually refer to." According to Archbishop Williams, we must remember the point of doctrine is to hold us still, to create a depth in us, "a space for radical change in how we think of ourselves and how we act."

When "Incarnation" names a mere set of beliefs, we are tempted, for example, to think "I thirst" must be said by the "very man" of the One who is "very God, very man." It is as if we think that what it means for Jesus to be very God and very man is that he was fifty percent God and fifty percent man. That is, Jesus must be half God and half man. But by the "Incarnation" the church refuses such a division, insisting that Jesus is at once one hundred percent God and one hundred percent man. The One who is the one God, very God and very man, is the One who thirsts.

That Jesus does thirst, moreover, is a reminder that "Incarnation" names a real and particular life. We rightly honor Mary's "Do with me what you will." We rightly celebrate the conception and birth of our Lord. If God is not in Mary's belly, we are not saved. But the One so conceived is the same One who has work to do on our behalf. His obedience matters, and it is an obedience that costs. He has a cup to drink, but it is the cup of death. We know the costs from Jesus's struggle with the devil in the wilderness as well as his prayer in Gethsemane that this cup be removed. But the cup cannot be removed if we are to be saved from the dryness that is our lives.

In Jesus's "I thirst" we confront again our desire to have a God that would not save us by a cross. We keep hoping that if the One who suffers on the cross is in some way connected to God, then there must be some remainder, there must be something saved in reserve: that the God who thirsts will find a way to escape from the cross. Surely the Son is not the Father, but we know from the Gospel of John that Jesus avows that what the Father has given him "is greater than all else, and no one can snatch it out of the Father's hand. The Father and I are one" (John 10:29–30). "Trinity" does not name a god who is something other than fully present in the Incarnation. Instead, without the Incarnation we would not have known the Father's love of the Son through the Spirit.

The work of the Son, the thirst of the Son through the Spirit, is nothing less than the Father's thirst for us. God desires us to desire God. We were created to thirst for God (Psalm 42) in a "dry and weary land where there is no water" (Psalm 63). Such a desire is as "physical" or real as our thirst for water, our thirst for one another, and our desire for God. Surely that is why our most determinative response to those who ask how we can ever come to worship this Jesus is to simply ask, "Do you not need to eat and drink?" Our God, our thirsty God, is the One capable of saying to us: "Let anyone who is thirsty come to me, and let the one who believes in me drink. As the scripture has said, 'Out of the believer's heart shall flow rivers of living water'" (John 7:37–38).

Through the waters of baptism we have been made God's body for the world. We thirst for one another so that the world may know that the world has been redeemed and that this redemption is as real as the water we need to survive. That redemption is found in the body and blood of our Lord that forever slakes our thirst. So refreshed, we become for the world the reminder that God has not abandoned us, and we can, therefore, trust in his promise that just to the extent we take the time—in a world that believes it has no time—to care for those who thirst for God's kingdom, the kingdom will be present.

six

The Sixth Word

"It is finished."

I t is finished" is not a death gurgle. "It is finished" is
not "I am done for." "It is finished" will not be, as we
know from the tradition of the ordering of these words
from the cross, the last words of Jesus. "It is finished" is
a cry of victory. "It is finished" is the triumphant cry that

what I came to do has been done. All is accomplished, completed, fulfilled work.

The work that is finished, moreover, is the cross. He will be and is resurrected, but the resurrected One remains the One crucified. Rowan Williams reminds us of Pascal's stark remark that "Jesus will be in agony until the end of the world." This is a remark that makes unavoidable the recognition that we live in the time between the times—the kingdom is begun in Christ but will not be consummated or perfected until the end of the world. Williams observes that Pascal's comment on Jesus's ongoing agony is not an observation about the deplorable state of unbelievers; it is instead an exhortation to us, those who believe in Christ. It is an exhortation not to become nostalgic for a supposedly less compromised past or take refuge in some imagined purified future, but to dwell in the tension-filled time between times, to remain awake to our inability "to stay in the almost unbearable present moment where Jesus is."

The Gospel of John makes explicit what all the Gospels assume—that is, the cross is not a defeat but the victory of our God. Earlier in the Gospel of John a voice from heaven responded to Jesus's request that the Father's name might be glorified through his obedience, saying

"I have glorified it, and I will glorify it again." Jesus tells us this voice came for our sake so that we might know that "Now is the judgement of this world; now the ruler of this world will be driven out. And I, when I am lifted up from the earth, will draw all people to myself" (John 12:28–32). That "lifting up" is the cross, the exaltation of the Son by the Father, making possible our salvation.

This is, moreover, as Pilate insisted, the King of the Jews. That kingship is not delayed by crucifixion; rather, crucifixion is the way this king rules. Crucifixion is kingdom come. This is the great long-awaited apocalyptic moment. Here the powers of this world are forever subverted. Time is now redeemed through the raising up of Jesus on this cross. A new age has begun. The kingdom is here aborn, a new regime is inaugurated, creating a new way of life for those who worship and follow Jesus.

Creation rightly describes the work done here. In his book *Believing Three Ways in the One God*, Nicholas Lash calls attention to a remark in a fifth-century calendar on March 25, a day identified as the martyrology of Jerome, which says, "Our Lord Jesus Christ was crucified, and conceived, and the world was made." Lash observes on this day, the day of crucifixion, God brings all things alive, creating *ex nihilo*, making a home in our sin-scarred world. "Out of the virgin's womb, Christ is conceived. Out of that world-threatening death on Calvary, life is new-born from an empty tomb. Christ's terror is God's Word's human vulnerability. But, it is just this vulnerability, this surrender, absolute relationship, which draws out of darkness finished life, forgiveness of sins."

On the sixth day of creation "God saw everything that he had made, and indeed, it was very good" (Genesis 1:31). So on the seventh day "God finished the work that he had done, and he rested on the seventh day from all the work that he had done" (Genesis 2:2). Accordingly the seventh day was hallowed. But God's work, the work of the Trinity, is consummated in Jesus's great declaration from the cross, "It is finished." His life, his death, his resurrection, as Irenaeus insisted, recapitulates creation, recapitulates God's covenant with Israel, uniting creation and redemption in Incarnation.

At the beginning of the Gospel of John we are told:

In the beginning was the Word, and the Word was with God, and the Word was God. He was in the beginning with God. All things came into being through him, and without him not one thing came into being. What has come into being in him was life, and the life was the light of all people. The light shines in the darkness, and the darkness did not overcome it. (John 1:1–5)

Creation has an end, creation is to be consummated, and the name of that end and consummation is Jesus.

Sin does not and cannot determine the character of Jesus's task. To be sure, he has come that we might be redeemed, but our redemption is but one movement in this drama of the beginning and end of time. In his book *After the Spirit*, Gene Rogers suggests that we let "redemption" name a plot defined by a starting point. We begin in slavery from which we are redeemed. The plot of consummation, however, is not determined by a starting point but by an endpoint: "it ends in joy, in *that to whom* one is united." Consummation is joy made possible by God's love, by God's friendship with us. In Jesus, redemption and consummation become movements in the one story of God's unrelenting love for his creation. That we—that is, we Gentiles—are included in the redemption of Israel is but a sign of the abundance of God's love and the completion of the new creation.

That is why "It is finished" is such good news. For Irenaeus, Jesus is the one who recapitulates all that God has done on our behalf until the final consummation. But this means that in Christ that recapitulation continues in the world. We, the body of Christ, through the Spirit, turn out to be "the finished." This, I believe, is what Athanasius meant by his dictum that God became human so that humans might become divine. Which means, as Richard Neuhaus puts it in his reflections on the seven words in his *Death on a Friday Afternoon*: "'It is finished.' But it is not over." God remains at work making us, his creatures, divine.

What is over is our vain attempts to be our own creators. What has happened is our overwhelming, says David Ford. We are overwhelmed by God's love through which we are able to see the beauty of God's care for all that is. Now it is possible for us to live at peace, to be God's agent of reconciliation, in a violent world. We are able so to live not because we have answers to all the world's troubles, but because God has given us a way to live without answers.

To so live does not mean we will be free of suffering, but it means that we can now live knowing it is through suffering that God's kingdom is manifest. Paul writes to the Colossians,

I am now rejoicing in my sufferings for your sake, and in my flesh I am completing what is lacking in Christ's afflictions for the sake of the body, that is, the church. I became its servant according to God's commission that was given to me for you, to make the word of God fully known, the mystery that has been hidden throughout the ages and generations but has now been revealed to his saints. To them God chose to make known how great among the Gentiles are the riches of the glory of this mystery, which is Christ in you, the hope of glory. (Colossians 1:24–27)

Paul is not suggesting that he must continue to suffer because Jesus's suffering on the cross was insufficient. On the contrary, Paul is able to suffer because the work of the cross is finished. Christ is triumphant. In the cross we see the image of the invisible God, the One in whom all things in heaven and on earth, visible and invisible, all thrones, dominions, rulers and powers, were created. He is the One who was before all things, and it is in him all things hold together. Accordingly he has become "the head of the body, the church; he is the beginning, the firstborn from the dead, so that he might come to have first place in everything. For in him all the fullness of God was pleased to dwell, and through him God was pleased to reconcile to himself all things, whether on earth or in heaven, by making peace through the blood of his cross" (Colossians 1:18–20).

God has finished what only God could finish. Christ's sacrifice is a gift that exceeds every debt. Our sins have been consumed, making possible lives that glow with the beauty of God's Spirit. What wonderful news: "'It is finished.' But it is not over." It is not over because God made us, the church, the "not over." We are made witnesses so the world—a world with no time for a crucified God—may know we have all the time of God's kingdom to live in peace with one another.

7

The Seventh Word

"Father, into your hands I commend my spirit."

These words, "Father, into thy hands I commend my spirit," have been repeated by countless Christians on their way to death. We Anglicans pray, at the Commendation in the Liturgy for Burial, "Into thy hands, O merciful Savior, we commend thy servant." Christians repeat these words in imitation of Jesus and because we assume these are words of comfort as we face the unknown that death names. These words can and should comfort, but that these words comfort us should not hide from us that these last words of Jesus before his death name his willingness to embrace the ice-cold silence of hell. Accordingly these words, "Father, into thy hands I commend my spirit," are every bit as frightening as Jesus's prior cry of abandonment. Jesus is not comforting himself; he is gesturing to the Father that he is ready to face the final work that only Jesus can do.

Jesus began his time on the cross praying to his Father. We should, therefore, not be surprised as his death draws near that he again prays as only the Son of God can pray. He prays to the Father. This should remind us that we can only imitate Jesus's prayer. We can repeat his words only because Jesus had no one to imitate. Jesus is the Christ, but the Christ is known only in the one called Jesus. Jesus is not a "Christ-figure" if by Christ-figure we mean the exemplification of a universal pattern of sacrifice for the goods of others. Jesus is no "Christ-figure" if we mean that his death is an exemplification of how we should all die; that is, we should die with the confidence that we have nothing to fear from death. No, this is the real and specific death of Jesus, the Savior of all that has been, is, and is to come, who submits to death by our hands—"Having said this he breathed his last." Dead. Jesus is dead.

We are told in John 1:18 that without the Son no one can see the Father. Von Balthasar, therefore, reminds us "when the Son, the Word of the Father is dead, then no one can see God, hear of him or attain him. And this day exists, when the Son is dead, and the Father, accordingly, inaccessible." This is the terror, the silence of the Father, to which Jesus has committed himself, this is why he cried the cry of abandonment. He has commended himself to the Father so he might for us undergo the dark night of death. Jesus commends himself to the Father, becoming for us all that is contrary to God. Christ suffers by becoming the "No" that the salvation wrought by his life creates. Without Christ there could be no hell—no abandonment by God—but the very hell created by Christ cannot overwhelm the love he has for us.

Jesus is really dead. He is on his way to Holy Saturday. Hell will be harrowed. Jesus goes to those who dwell in isolation from themselves, one another, and God to overcome the silence of their lives. He is the Word who alone can make communication possible between those who can speak but not hear. Only the Son of God is capable of this task, that is, to submit fully to death and yet redeem the destruction death names. For this the Son of God came, to assume our nature, making possible the proclamation of the gospel, as we are told in 1 Peter 4:6, "even to the dead, so that, though they had been judged in the flesh as everyone is judged, they might live in the spirit as God does." Because Jesus, the Son of God, has done this great work, he can tell us in the book of Revelation: "'Do not be afraid; I am the first and the last, and the living one. I was dead, and see, I am alive forever and ever; and I have the keys of Death and of Hades'" (Revelation 1:17–18).

This great work makes possible our baptism into his life and into his death. By giving himself up and commending his spirit to the Father, Jesus invites and enables us to give ourselves up and become "united with him in a death like his" (Romans 6:5). Through baptism we are inducted into Jesus's death and life. We are made part of God's great eschatological drama—a cosmic drama in which the whole land was covered with darkness because the very light of the sun failed. Even the curtain in the temple was torn in two. For Jesus Christ was:

> put to death in the flesh, but made alive in the spirit, in
> which also he went and made a proclamation to the spirits

in prison, who in former times did not obey, when God waited patiently in the days of Noah, during the building of the ark, in which a few . . . were saved through water. And baptism, which this prefigured, now saves you—not as a removal of dirt from the body, but as an appeal to God for a good conscience, through the resurrection of Jesus Christ, who has gone into heaven and is at the right hand of God, with angels, authorities, and powers made subject to him. (1 Peter 3:18–22)

Christ had no Christ to imitate, but we also know, as we have just heard from 1 Peter and from the Psalms, that what he has done has been anticipated. These words, "Father into your hands I commit my spirit," are prayed by the psalmist:

> You are indeed my rock and my
>   fortress;
>   for your name's sake lead me
>   and guide me,
> take me out of the net that is
>   hidden for me,
>   for you are my refuge.
> Into your hand I commit my
>   spirit;

you have redeemed me,
O LORD, faithful God. (Psalm 31:3–5)

Only now, that is, with Jesus's death, do we begin to understand what we pray and sing when we pray and sing the Psalms. In the Psalms we are invited to complain:

How long, O LORD? Will you
forget me forever?
How long will you hide your
face from me?
How long must I bear pain in
my soul,
and have sorrow in my heart
all day long?
How long shall my enemy be
exalted over me?

The psalmist refuses to lie. God's covenant with Israel has tested her. Israel has sinned and been judged, leaving her with no illusions. The psalmist is blunt—God does not remember, God does not make things right.

Consider and answer me,
O LORD my God!

> Give light to my eyes, or I will
>   sleep the sleep of death,
> and my enemy will say, "I have
>   prevailed";
> my foes will rejoice because I
>   am shaken.

Yet the psalmist, Israel, rejoices. Israel rejoices even though her enemies triumph, illness threatens, her children suffer, and death is sure.

> But I trusted in your steadfast
>   love;
>   my heart shall rejoice in your
>   salvation.
> I will sing to the LORD,
>   because he has dealt
>   bountifully with me. (Psalm 13)

Jesus has become the Father's Psalm for the world, fulfilling Israel's undying hope that death, and the judgment death must be and always is, is not the last word. According to Christopher Seitz, God has become for us death, destroying "whatever gap we might have suspected existed

between God and his complete disclosure of himself to us."
Jesus commits himself fully to the Father, a sorrowful com-
mitment to the death, thereby joining us to his promised
people, Israel.

Like Israel, like the Jews, we will be persecuted, we will
suffer, we will die. But because of what Jesus has done
on this cross, we will be able to die confidently praying: "Father, into your hands I commit my spirit." Such
a prayer can be prayed because we have witnesses like
Christian de Cherge, who are for us bodily reminders that
Christ has triumphed through the cross. Such a prayer
can be made because Christ's promise to a thief is also his
promise to us. Such a prayer can be said because Mary
said, "Here am I." Such a prayer can be made because we
know that Jesus fully and willingly shared our existence,
accepting even the judgment our sins required.

So come, draw near, fear not, and behold the mystery
and the wonder of Jesus's cross.

Bibliography

Augustine, sermon 169, 11, 13.

Cantalamessa, Raniero. *Mary: Mirror of the Church*. Collegeville, MN: Liturgical Press, 1992.

Ford, David F. *The Shape of Living: Spiritual Direction for Everyday Life*. Grand Rapids: Baker, 1997.

Hanby, Michael. "War on Ash Wednesday: A Brief Christological Reflection." *New Blackfriars* 84/986 (April 2003): 168–78.

Hart, David. *The Beauty of the Infinite: The Aesthetics of Christian Truth*. Grand Rapids: Eerdmans, 2003.

James, William. *The Varieties of Religious Experience*. New York: Mentor, 1958.

Kiser, John W. *Monks of Tibhirine*. New York: St. Martin's, 2002.

Lash, Nicholas. *Believing Three Ways in One God: A Reading of the Apostles Creed*. Notre Dame, IN: University of Notre Dame Press, 1993.

McCabe, Herbert, OP. *God Still Matters*. London: Continuum, 2002.

Neuhaus, Richard John. *Death on a Friday Afternoon: Meditations on the Last Words of Jesus from the Cross*. New York: Basic Books, 2000.

Rogers, Eugene. *After the Spirit*. Grand Rapids: Eerdmans, 2005.

Seitz, Christopher. *Seven Lasting Words: Jesus Speaks from the Cross*. Louisville: Westminster John Knox, 2001.

Turner, Denys. "On Denying the Right God: Aquinas on Atheism and Idolatry." *Modern Theology* 20/1 (January 2004): 141–62.

von Balthasar, Hans Urs. *Mysterium Paschale*, translated with an introduction by Aidan Nichols, O.P. Grand Rapids: Eerdmans, 1990.

Williams, Rowan. *Anglican Identities*. Cambridge, MA: Cowley, 2003.

———. *Christ on Trial: How the Gospel Unsettles Our Judgment*. London: HarperCollins, 2000.

On Creating the Artwork
for This Book

C*ross-Shattered Christ* helped take me deeper into Jesus again. I don't really like going to the cross—I usually feel like the man who was forced into carrying Jesus's cross with him. And yet I know I need to keep going to the cross because every time I do I get a little more free. So for the artist, a project like this becomes a kind of spiritual exercise. Searching for images and refining them actually carries me deeper into the presence of God. My prayer and hope is that the pictures for this book would reinforce what God wants to say through Stanley Hauerwas's meditations.

Because I am such a visual person, a manuscript of pure text and no pictures makes me dizzy at first, just sort of swims in front of me as my eyes try to focus but can't. So with a project like this I begin with a simple prayer for God's help and then I read a little bit at a time. Then I read the same thing over and over again. As I do this I make some very simple pencil drawings of images that float to the surface. These beginning drawings are very clumsy and crude and in fact sometimes don't even relate very closely to the text. As an example, what I first came up with for Jesus's cry of thirst was a sponge soaked with wine on the end of a spear. But as I reflected on Hauerwas's observations I began to think of these words in the context of Jesus's desire for relationship with us. I let the drawings develop along new paths as they continued to evolve, as I tried different combinations, different compositions. I also did some library research and brought home about sixty pounds of oversized art history books to help me get inspired. I really can't create in a vacuum. I need inspiring pictures and objects around me.

These pictures were done in wood block printing process. The process begins with the pencil sketches just described. There is kind of a mysterious transformation when you go from drawing to the block print, because one medium is so different from the other. With a pencil you just lightly drag the lead over the paper and you immediately have a mark. But for a woodcut you are actually carving into a smooth block of wood that will later be inked and pressed with paper to receive an impression, a process that is much less direct and immediate than drawing. Also, the wood resists your carving, and the wood grain wants to take your knife in its own direction. By such means the medium adds its own uniqueness to each finished image.

When I get the drawn design completed, I transfer the drawings with a white colored pencil onto a block of birch plywood that has been painted black. The next step is to carve out the negative spaces where the block will not print, leaving the raised surface to receive the ink and print black. This process of making a printed image is very simple and unchanged for thousands of years. The result is always something stark and primitive, something that stands out among the glut of slick images we are now bombarded with daily.

I was honored to be invited into this project. Perhaps, with our culture all the time becoming more visually oriented, we may some day find ourselves returning to the illuminated manuscript.

RICK BEERHORST